Poetry of Three Generations

An Anthology of Poems
Leonard Milgraum
Michael Milgraum
Rena Milgraum

Guidelight Books
9525 Georgia Avenue, Suite 203
Silver Spring, MD 20910
guidelightbooks@gmail.com

To Sylvia, my inspiration,
My four unique children—Sandy, Candy, Randy and Michael,
The grandchildren and great-grandchildren—my ever-increasing
treasures, and
God, who has given me all this.

—L.M.

To Hirsh, Shayna, Rena, and Chana—our future

—M.M.

To Atara

—R.M.

Contents

Poetry
of
Three Generations

Foreword

Words have magic, words create. Every child knows that the wizard has to chant the vital words for each spell to occur. And, as the Bible says, there was only darkness until God said, "Let there be light." My father taught me the power of words, how they can warm or wound the soul, how they can be our most powerful tools or our most insurmountable obstacles. My earliest memories are of my father singing his wonderful songs with their delightful lyrics and filling our lives with playfulness and joy. (Some of these songs were his own compositions, others were from popular music.) His love for music and its rhythms have infused his poetry, as he has scribbled on his legal pad, with his felt-tipped pen, for more than seventy years. His poetry taught me that one could use very few words to say much and that those few words often had more power than more embellished speech. His poetry and his insights, throughout the years, have also taught me that the one who speaks and writes creates a vision for himself and for others. It is a vision that is essential for us to know who we are, where we are and where we are going.

It was my father's passion for writing that inspired me to find my own voice and share my thoughts and my vision with the world. In the busy rush and tumble of life, it has often been very challenging to find time for writing, but I have somehow squeezed it in. I have written to express emotion, challenge myself and remind myself of what is most important.

Strangely enough, I was somehow not prepared for how this love for words would impact the next generation—my own children. When my daughter, Rena, started to compose her own poetry, at age eleven, I encountered her in a new way. In her poems, I heard a depth of spirit and a maturity of expression that I could not believe originated in one so young. Rena had absorbed her heritage and dived into the world of writing. She had found her voice. It would not be accurate to say I was proud; it was much deeper than that. I guess I will say that I felt blessed.

The title *Poetry of Three Generations* was Rena's idea. I hope that this book will inspire young writers, like Rena, to seek their voice, create, and be awed by the power of words.

Michael Milgraum
Silver Spring, Maryland
January 15, 2013

A Parable About
Rhythm, Music, Words and Spirit

This parable is based on a story that occurs in Chapter 9 of Genesis. The story relates that after the great flood, Noah planted a vineyard, became drunk, and was naked in his tent. Noah had three sons. The eldest was Japheth, the middle was Shem, and the youngest was Ham. Ham was the father of Canaan. Ham saw his father in this compromised condition and went to tell his two brothers. Shem and Japheth then took a garment, placed it on their shoulders, and walked backwards, so as not to see their father, as they covered him. When Noah awoke from his drunkenness, he had the following to say, "Cursed be Canaan, a servant of servants shall he be unto his brethren...Blessed be the Lord, God of Shem, and Canaan shall be their servant. May God expand Japheth, and may He dwell in the tents of Shem, and may Canaan be a slave to them."

In Jewish thought, each one of these brother's names is related to their characters. Ham, which means "heat" in Hebrew, was a seeker of physical pleasure (driven by the "heat" of human desire). Japheth, which means "beauty," was drawn to esthetic and artistic pursuits. Shem, which means "name," was devoted to the intellect and spirituality—he would use "names" (words) to reach beyond the mundane of our five senses.

Jewish sources further explain that Ham brought disfavor on himself and his progeny because he mocked his father upon discovering him in his humiliated state, and made no effort to help him. It was the two older brothers that took steps to restore honor to their father. (Canaan, the son of Ham, is cursed in order to emphasize that he continued in his father's ways).

In truth, the three traits that Japheth, Shem and Ham represent can be found, to varying degrees, in each one of us. Physical desire, longing for esthetic beauty and spirituality vie together in the heart of each man. If these forces are at odds, much destruction can ensue. The parable below presents an alternative.

❖   ❖   ❖

There once was a king who had three sons. The middle son was the most serious and studious. The eldest son did adequately at his studies, but spent too much time dozing away in the royal orchard and feasting on its delicious fruit. The youngest son was mischievous and was always in trouble. He constantly avoided his studies, and stayed out late, getting drunk with his friends. He often hid in the graveyard and jumped out to scare passersby in the middle of the night.

One day the king called the youngest son to him and said "Son, this is no way to be. If you can make no good use of what I have offered you here, then you must leave and seek your fortune elsewhere... And don't return until you have found something new and useful to bring back with you."

So the young man traveled far and wide. He saw many things, some that were new, some that were useful, but none that were both. Finally, he came to the Land of the Drums. The young man had never seen or heard drums before, because there were none in his kingdom. The natives in the Land of the Drums would play the most compelling rhythms, which would cause all to dance with wild abandon. The young man became intoxicated with these rhythms and spent a year living in the Land of the Drums, dancing to the rhythms and learning how to beat them out himself. Finally, after the year had passed, the young man became homesick. He acquired a drum and set out to bring it back to the kingdom, to share what he had found.

However, shortly before his return, the king had started to worry about him. The king called for his eldest son and bid him to go and search for the youngest son and to inquire into his welfare.

One month after the eldest son departed, the youngest son returned. He went directly to the king, who asked him, with a stern face, "So, son, have you brought back something new and useful?" In response to his question, the son started to beat on his drum. The rhythms were intoxicating to all who heard them. As the son continued to play, more and more people were drawn to the king's palace by the beat. The people danced a wild dance and forgot about their daily chores, responsibilities and routines. Teachers did not teach, farmers did not plow, blacksmiths did not light their fires, bakers did not bake and no one collected the eggs or milked the cows. The only thing anyone wanted to do was dance to the beat. The dancing continued, day after day, for many months.

Meanwhile, the eldest son traveled to many lands, seeking the youngest son. He finally came to the Land of the Drums and received news about his brother. He stayed there for a few days, but became bored with the incessant beat—he wanted something more. He journeyed on and came across the Land of Music. The Land of Music had perfected the art of music, played on the most beautiful instruments, and the young man was entranced by the music, because there was no music in his kingdom. He decided to stay for a while in the Land of Music. Week followed week, and he stayed in the land of music for one year. He devotedly studied the art of music and found himself quite talented at it. Finally, the son remembered his father and set out (carrying his harp) to return to the kingdom.

Meanwhile, the king was becoming concerned about his eldest son. He called the middle son to him (this son was the only one who had continued productive activity—his studies—during the time of the drums). The king told the son to go out of the kingdom to seek his brother and bring back word of his welfare.

Shortly after the middle son departed, the eldest son returned. He found the kingdom in shambles. Buildings were collapsing because no one would repair them, and all the wild dancing had broken many floors. Intuitively knowing what he had to do, the eldest son brought his harp to the market place and began to play. Almost instantly, the soul of each dancer was soothed. The people calmed down and no longer yearned for their wild dance. Teachers began to teach, farmers began to plow, blacksmiths lit their fires, the mountains of eggs were cleaned up and the cows were finally tended to and milked.

The people so loved this new thing called "music" that they would look forward to the evening with great anticipation, when they would gather and listen to the beautiful harp, accompanied by the stirring rhythm of the drums. When they were played together, the harp soothed and the drums excited, creating a perfect balance. The people felt a warm, sustaining glow within them. Everything was back to how it should be—except for one thing. The people were so mystified by the music that they forgot about each other. Friends no longer came to visit one another. No one gave charity to the needy. No one visited the sick. "We have no more need for kindness," the people thought. "We have music to warm our souls."

Meanwhile, the middle son was traveling far away. He came to the Land of the Drums, found it to be too wild for his tastes, and traveled on. He came to the Land of Music, as well. He stayed there for a few days, enjoying the lovely tunes. But he then remembered his father's charge and traveled on. Finally, he came to the Land of the Name. Now, this was a place unlike any he had seen before. The inhabitants devoted all their time to a most marvelous and uplifting pursuit.

They explained their activities to the young man by telling him a story: When God created the world, He wanted to take some of His goodness, love and power and fill up the world with it. However, when He tried to do that, the world was unable to hold all of this powerful goodness, and the goodness shattered into billions of pieces and spread all over the world. The people in the Land of the Name devoted their time to putting pieces of this goodness back together, so that the world would be filled with a united good once more. The people did their work by meditating on the essence of each object in the world, and when they discovered its essence, they would know the proper name to give to it, a name that would properly contain this splinter of God's goodness. After they discovered this name, they would include it in poetry they composed. It was these poems which stitched together the shattered pieces of God's goodness.

The son wanted to return to his father, to complete the charge. But he also realized that perhaps, in a deeper way, he needed to stay, all the more so to fulfill his father's charge. The son realized that somehow the spark of God that had been placed in his youngest brother had become splintered and separated from the rest of the good. Perhaps the teachings of this land could provide a way to return it home.

The middle son stayed in the Land of the Name for five years, learning its secrets. After delving into the true depths of its wisdom, he discovered the true name for his younger brother—it was "Fire." Also, in his meditation, the true name of his older brother came to him—it was "Beauty." And finally his own name came to him—it was "Name." When the son realized his own name, he knew he was ready to return home.

Upon his return, he found the people much calmed—compared to how he left them—but he was astounded by how heartless they had become.

So he called out from the center of the palace with these words:

> "Let Fire, Beauty and Name unite.
> To bring back home the shattered light,
> A vessel for the One above.
> We only live where there is love."

Suddenly, all eyes turned to the palace. All hearts were drawn there. And from that day on, the youngest son would play his drums, the eldest his harp and the middle son would sing along with words of spirit and power, words that made the people compassionate and good. Great prosperity came to the kingdom, and it was blessed with peace.

—Michael Milgraum

PARENTS
AND CHILDREN

∝ The Graduate

I cannot take one step for you
Along the path of truth.
I may provide a hint, a clue,
A story from my youth.

Yet all of this is from my road,
My triumphs and travail.
It cannot lighten up your load,
Or see that you prevail.

You must be ready to receive
The message deep within.
You must awaken to believe
The sounds beyond the din.

To each of us the spirit calls,
Invisible commands,
Tugging on our inner walls,
Flowing, Braille-like hands.

Listen with an open heart,
Joyful in the dance.
Become a worthy work of art,
A rollicking romance.

Triumph over gloom and pain.
Flower like a rose.
Touch the thorn and taste the rain,
Relishing life's blows.

There'll never be another you,
A miracle to know.

My love's too deep to smother you,
But it hurts to let you go.

And yet I do, for deep inside,
I would not make you stay.
Enraptured in parental pride,
Wistfully I watch you walk away.

—Leonard Milgraum

❧ A Baby

A warm, little bundle,
A tiny life,
Right there in your arms.

Yet to grow,
Yet to know,
Right there in your arms.

Destined for strife,
Destined for life,
Right there in your arms.

To laugh and to cry,
To smile and to sigh,
Right there in your arms.

Product of love,
A gift from above,
Right there in your arms.

—Rena Milgraum

℘ My Baby

I come home from the hospital,
A bundle in my arms,
Exhausted, weak, yet overjoyed,
Your tiny form, my comfort.

Adventure 'round every corner.
Growing every day.
Aware of the world around you,
You learn, you grow, you change.

Your first teeth, first words, first steps,
First time climbing up the stairs,
Every moment a new experience,
Every second a surprise.

Your first haircut, first real bed,
First time climbing out of your crib,
Time flying past too quickly,
You learn, you grow, you change.

Your first playgroup, first play date,
First time skipping your nap,
You're growing out of diapers,
Your favorite word is "NO!"

Everything is luxury,
Yet somehow it is not,
I'm missing how you're growing up,
You learn, you grow, you change.

Your first birthday party, first trip to the mall,
First real year in school,

You love your school, you're making friends,
You're a lovable, strong-willed child.

Meanwhile, I push my troubles away,
And try to live in the now,
Just enjoying being a mother.
You learn, you grow, you change.

Your first pet, first time riding a horse,
First time learning your times tables,
Less new happenings, and more of the old,
Falling into a graceful pattern.

You love to ice skate, your running is stupendous.
All your clothing is getting too small.
And still I push away my worries.
You learn, you grow, you change.

First time in middle school,
But all else mostly the same,
You're becoming a teenager,
And I wish you were still young.

Wasn't it just yesterday when you began to talk?
I truly miss those baby years.
When your warm head rested on my chest,
You learn, you grow, you change.

Your first year in high school,
First time with a phone,
Now you're getting way too old,
And I don't understand it.

The tears of joy I shed, from raising you from a baby,
Are mixed with tears of sadness too,
Of how that baby is gone.
You learn, you grow, you change.

Your first year in college,
Keeping your eye out for your match,
I can't bear you being away from me,
I wish you'd never left.

Yet, still I know it's for the best,
You need to live your life,
But pain shoots through my heart when I think,
Where has my baby gone?
You learn, you grow, you change.

You're married now. The house so quiet,
Nothing seems the same.
This time I know you live here no more,
I wish you would come back.

You have your own life now,
You visit from time to time,
But you're a new person now, with a confident air,
You learn, you grow, you change.

But as time goes on I'm happy,
Happier than I thought I ever would be,
I have children, grandchildren and great ones too,
For now I know that when you let go, they always come
    back with more.

—Rena Milgraum

❧ *Little One*

Ah, itty bitty ball of becoming—
Fetal floating in your lair,
Soon to set the earth ahumming,
Coming forth alive, aware.

Endless joy in your arrival,
Momma's pain a blurring blot,
All concerned for your survival,
Cuddling the tender tot.

Ah, what smiles, what exultation,
Oh, what promise lies ahead,
From cradle right through graduation,
Oh, the light that you will shed.

Product of your parents' caring,
Dividend of love divine,
Lead your people with your daring,
As you shed your special shine.

Mom and Dad, I would beseech you,
To observe your tiny guest.
The little one has much to teach you.
Listen, learn and love with zest.

—Leonard Milgraum

ℭℜ

Tell me "once upon a time,"
So I'll retrace my years,
When innocent and quite sublime
The present disappears.

And once more wonder fills my heart
And fairy tales come true.
Crayon scribbling is an art
And every dawn seems new.

Modern life's a growing gale
With howling winds of war.
Please tell me one more fairy tale
So I'll feel safe once more.

—Leonard Milgraum

CR

I told my son, "You must obey."
He rolled his eyes and walked away.
I followed, said "Don't mess with me,
For I have power, you will see."

I crafted schemes, made plans complete,
So clever in my full conceit—
A carrot to draw him to my demand,
A stick to chase him from his stand.

But what I did not understand
Is, as a boy becomes a man,
His passion is to be like me,
His power, he wants us both to see.

The more I pushed, the more resistance.
The more I fumed, the more indifference.
My threats increased, to no avail.
I knew, inside my heart, I'd failed.

Face to face, defiant, we
Each other could no longer see.

I told my son I heard his voice,
I recognized his power of choice.
He, skeptical, believing not,
Thought this might be another plot.

But I had changed. A different view
Inside I held of him, me too.
My place: to guide, not to control,
Much more to love, much less to scold.

21

No longer slave to strategy,
I strove to let my love flow free.
The truth, in time, will always win.
True love, it penetrated him.

And now we talk and smile and play
It helps us grow, from day to day.

—Michael Milgraum

છ

What is the world in which you reside?
I gaze in your eyes, but part of you hides.
You appear to have found a world I can't see,
A world that is foreign and distant from me.
Is it a dreamland or an actual place?
I study your speaking, I stare at your face.
A face that I've loved from the moment of birth,
A spirited bubble unique to this earth.
Everyone seeks for their own special space
To ponder their purpose, their meaning, their base.
No need to explain, you've a right to your choice.
I taught you to follow your own special voice.
While I don't understand, I am truly beguiled.
May you find deep fulfillment and peace, my dear child.

—Leonard Milgraum

❧ To Mom on Her Seventieth Birthday

Life gives and takes
I strive and ache,
I fall and rise again.
I make a map,
But that gets scrapped.
I try another plan.

Through hopes and dreams,
Through many schemes,
I wend my wandering way.
My challenge clear,
And always near,
Is but to LIVE each day.

The gift you gave—
A heart that's brave
To frankly face each day,
In service true,
You gave of *you*,
And how can I repay?

Four children
God has gifted me.
My love I give to them.
I wipe their tears.
I hear their fears…
Your love is without end.

The seed you've sown,
The love that's grown
In me, I give to them,

And they'll give to
Their children who
Will give this love again.

The greatest praise
The brightest rays
Of light in you I see,
'Twas you raised me
In love to be
A giver once again.

—Michael Milgraum

I wrote this poem after three years of working as a psychologist with inner city youth.

☙ From Boys to Men

From men to boys,
From boys to men,
The generations go again.
Who's an enemy?
Who's a friend?
From men to boys,
From boys to men.

The sun comes up.
The sun goes down.
Do things change as years go 'round?
Can you make a different sound
From those who lie beneath the ground?
The sun comes up.
The sun goes down.

You threaten me.
I threaten you.
And one will fall before we're through.
But fallen ones will strike back too.
You threaten me.
I threaten you.

From hate to hurt,
From hurt to hate.
The strong survive; the weak ones wait,
That some will care about their fate.
From hate to hurt,
From hurt to hate.

As fathers do,
So children see
Or do not see, but hear, maybe
Of lives lost behind the jailer's key.
As fathers do,
So children see.

They can't relax.
They can't let go.
A puff of smoke is all they know
To ease the pain they will not show.
They can't relax.
They can't let go.

The future children
Understand
That their lives lay
In these young men's hands
To choose each day
To hope or hate,
To work or shirk,
To jump or wait,
To respect or to reject,
To undo their father's neglect.
The future children understand
And they watch, questioning each young man.
From men to boys,
From boys to men.

—Michael Milgraum

THE ART OF LIVING

CR

A large dog saw a little pup
Chasing his tail round and round.
The older dog said, "Little pup, what's up?"
The little dog circled and frowned.

"I've studied and mastered philosophy.
I am brilliant at puzzles and chess.
My tail represents happiness to me.
Once I catch it I'll have happiness."

The older dog smiled,
"I too have a tale to relay.
Like my tail, happiness is elusive you see,
If I chase it, it just runs away.
As I go about my work it follows after me."

—Leonard Milgraum

◌◌ The Banquet of Man

Locked in the prison of yesterday's furies,
Chained to the patterns and pains of the past,
Pinioned by peers and the verdicts of juries,
Eye toward the future, false pride to the last.

Tossed between ego and scars of the mind view,
Fleeing from demons, while seeking hurrahs,
Race to escape what is lurking behind you,
Enslaved between jailers of "will be" and "was".

Missing the beauty of every sweet second,
Blind to the miracle free to the taste,
Deaf to the call of the wind while it beckoned,
Oceans of tears for the terrible waste.

Idiot's game of con and confusion,
Science must falter and fail us somehow.
Savor the present, all else is illusion.
Everything worthy is God, love and now.

Fate merely smiles while the foolish go scheming,
Tone-deaf to sound while the symphony plays,
Sleeping while waking and aching in the dreaming,
Lost to the rhythm of infinite days.

Drink in the sunshine and sip of the water.
Thrill to the air and the fruit of the land.
Kiss Mother Nature and dance with her daughter.
Study each bead of the shimmering sand.

Dare to be different, to be what you are—fine.
Walk in the way that your spirit be whole.

Open yourself to the light of a star shine.
Open your mind to the truth in your soul.

Escape from the dungeon of yesteryear's torment.
Laugh at tomorrow—a conjurer's jest.
Rekindle the fire within, lying dormant.
Life is a banquet in search of a guest.

—Leonard Milgraum

❧ Try With All Your Heart

Today, a six-year-old girl on monkey bars
Reminded me of something basic, something essential,
Something I've overlooked.

She said, "I know I can do it, I know I can.
All I need to do is try with all my heart."

And day after day the dull ache lives within me,
The disappointment with myself,
The self-absorption, the dull habits of avoidance,
Self-protection, self-sabotage and perfectionism.
And all the while, growing more hopeless and empty.
But then she said "try with all my heart"
And I remembered an inkling of a thought
Of a heart undivided
Where determination, hopefulness and will combine
And with a rush of adrenaline, I have climbed the
    insurmountable hill.

Of course not all challenges need such exertion.
In fact, sometimes the greatest challenge is to accept that
    less exertion would be fine.
But what is needed, and always will be, is an undivided
    heart.
Because an undivided heart
Sweeps away the despair of having tried a thousand
    times before
And says, just do it now and taste the sweetness of life.

"Try with all my heart," I say to myself.
I then announce to her that I will do the monkey bars
    "with all my heart"

And whereas a few minutes ago I hung in pain
And simply dropped, in order to protect my aching
   muscles,
Now, I grit my teeth and, arm by arm,
Work my way across,
Straining with my untrained arms
Not taking "no" for an answer.
I think tomorrow will be different,
Because today already is.

—Michael Milgraum

℘ Yoga

I inhale and exhale,
Every part of me relaxed,
Calming music playing,
I lower my arms and stretch.

Child's pose,
Oh what a feel,
Utmost relaxation,
Slowly I roll up and reach to touch my toes.

I feel the stretch,
Palms grip the mat,
I roll up and lie back,
I let my limbs lie limp, I close my eyes.

Ah, the wonders of the body,
How I can move, how I can run,
Refreshed, I open my eyes,
Disappointed that I am done.

—Rena Milgraum

∞ Jogging

Slush, crush, slosh, the leaves and mud,
Under foot, as pumping blood
Passes through my panting frame,
"Push the pace" flows through my brain.

Slowly climb this maddening hill
With a force of wish and will,
Crush, crush, crush the gravel sounds,
Progress slowed by moving ground.

Branches, roots and rocks speed by
Underneath the darkening sky.
Evening mists cloak all in white
Destination soon in sight.

Give your all, it's almost done.
This is why the race is run—
Proves my body still is there,
Straining muscles, wind-washed hair.

—Michael Milgraum

CR

Life is a journey we all get to begin
Without any road map for guide,
The ultimate pathways are hidden within,
As we travel from pleasure to pride.

Who can foresee all the brambles and brush,
All the byways that lead to no end.
Who can find peace midst the bluster and blush
And choose between villain and friend.

Onward we go from the twists and the turns
Encountering losses and wins.
Life is a blending of blessings and burns
Of courage in conquering sins.

As we approach our very last mile
To our eternal neighborhood,
Let us strive that each soul has a song and a smile
That we acted the best that we could.

—Leonard Milgraum

It isn't what happens, it's how you perceive it.
It isn't that action, it's how you react.
It's not the surprise, it's how you receive it.
Some comments are hard to retract.

The glass is half empty, or is it half full?
It lies in the eye of the beholder.
The string is ours alone to pull.
Am I old or just getting older?

Some just rage at each winter storm,
Cursing the snow and the frost,
Others bless their shelter so warm,
Build snowmen without any cost.

It is better to look for the good
Than dwell on the evil about.
Find peace at a pond, a walk in the wood,
A kiss or a hug, not a shout.

Courageously face disappointment.
Laugh every trouble away,
Using your smile as an ointment.
With your will you can brighten each day.

Some fear night's darkness and shiver
Some look for stars of all kind.
Depend on yourself to deliver
And the positive frame of your mind.

Remember it's all in your power.
Don't let others' actions be king.

Search for the sweet and sidestep the sour
Make your spirit control everything.

We all know how quickly it's over.
Let's brighten this moment somehow,
See not the weed but savor the clover,
Infused with the beauty of now.

—Leonard Milgraum

၄

Start off each day
With joy as you pray.
Smile in the shower and splash.

Breakfast with zest,
Know that you're blest.
Count your blessings instead of your cash.

So many folk
Think life's a mean joke
And each disappointment rehash.

Be battler, not boozer,
Envy's a loser.
Count your blessings instead of your cash.

Waste not your yearnings
To triple your earnings.
Don't grimace and make your teeth gnash.

Open your soul
To a much better goal.
Count your blessings instead of your cash.

Keep love alive,
Dream as you strive,
Lacing life's dance with panache.

Let others quest
And worship gold's chest.
You count your blessings instead of your cash.

For right at the end,
Money's never our friend.
We each bid adieu to our stash.

Count your true treasure
Every moment of pleasure.
Just count your blessings instead of your cash.

—Leonard Milgraum

Art

Art
Freedom
A choice of all creations

Art
Colors
Mix them, blend them, paint them

Art
Textures
Bumpy, scratchy, smooth

Art
Enjoy
Have fun while you make it

—Rena Milgraum

CR

The clouds have blotted out the sun,
A dark and dismal day,
A gloomy mood for everyone,
With winter on its way.

We knew the summer could not last,
Its warmth so quickly spent.
Its liveliness went by so fast,
A sparkling event.

It's hard to keep your spirit high
With sleet and snow ahead.
Summer's song becomes a sigh
With most the flowers dead.

Somehow we have to lift our sight,
Stretch our perception wide,
Search within to seek the light
And my love right by my side.

—Leonard Milgraum

The flowers bud and bloom, then fade,
A portion of life's puzzling parade.
The seasons come, the seasons go,
The summer's heat, the winter's snow,
Icy winds to freeze one's heart,
Sunsets glow—a work of art,
Floods that inundate the land,
A walk at dawn along the sand,
A fond embrace—a kindly act,
A senseless, brutal terrorist attack,
Endless hatred tribe to tribe,
A love poem written by a scribe,
The promise of a mother's birth,
An aged one who's laid to earth,
We wake, we eat, we work, we sleep,
And all the questions burrow deep.
The answers lie beyond our mind.
The purpose of all humankind
Is simply to act morally and strive
To serve our master while we're still alive.
So, when our soul departs its earthly lair
It's quite improved from when it first came here.

—Leonard Milgraum

CR

Every day is a miracle—a wonder to behold
A special priceless miracle—more valuable than gold.
Every day's a soulful song—a melody unique,
The magic of the moment—seven days each week.

From early dawn to setting sun,
Its grandeur's there for everyone.
To lavish in its gift of happiness
Away from all the worry and the stress.

Breathe deep and relish all its treasure.
Its simple songbirds bring us pleasure.
So open up your soul to the message of each day,
Your present is its presence—don't let it slip away.

—Leonard Milgraum

༃ *Poetry*

A waterfall of words,
Truth of inner feelings,
A way to express myself,
Words of truth and healing.

Nothing seems wrong with the world,
As I sit here with my pen.
My heart sending words through the ink,
My heart dropping words on the page.

I breathe in deep,
The smell of calm,
The welcoming silence—serene,
Not knowing what I will write next—
My heart dropping words on a page.

—Rena Milgraum

NATURE

❧ The Beach

Hot sand beneath me,
Sky above me,
Waves slapping on the shore.

Gulls are crying,
Wind is sighing,
Sun beating down upon me.

The warm, soft sand,
Within my hand,
The calming beauty, paradise.

The endless sand,
Reaches out a hand,
I take it and become nature.

Here I belong,
I sing a song,
To God who made it for me.

—Rena Milgraum

◌৪ *Nature 2*

When I see a tree cut down,
I feel pain shoot through my heart,
And I am cut down too.

When I see a lake polluted,
I can hear nature screaming,
And a piece of me screams too.

When I see an animal killed,
I am wounded through the heart,
And I am killed too.

When I see nature destroyed,
I feel eternal pain,
And a piece of me is destroyed too.

—Rena Milgraum

ᘓ

Does anything compare
To breathing fresh, clean air,
As you walk along a forest or shore,

Away from fumes and gases
And greedy lads and lasses,
Never knowing less is really more?

Heed your inner voice.
In the silence you'll rejoice.
In the stillness there is melody and verse.

A wisdom waiting for us,
If we listen to its chorus,
Eternal truths infuse the universe.

Let the quiet feed your soul,
A place to make your spirit whole,
The majesty in simply letting go.

Find serenity and calm
With one soul mate at your arm,
Proud to be in God's great fashion show.

It's not the clothes you wear
Or your nails and fancy hair
That makes you the true person that you are.

Out in nature we all shine,
Slowly meld with the divine.
Everyone can be a shining star.

—Leonard Milgraum

⊗ *An Ocean of Contentment*

The beach smells of calm as I survey its blue waters,
So vastly powerful, yet so infinitely calm,
I am drawn to the sounds that resound all around me,
As an ocean of contentment overflows in my heart.

I hear the rise and fall of the tide,
As it slowly moves up shore.
I hear the cawing of the occasional bird,
Mixed with the crying of the seagulls.
I hear the morning crickets chirping in harmony,
Singing me their daily song,
As an ocean of contentment overflows in my heart.

—Rena Milgraum

֍

I love to sit and slowly scan
The scene before my eyes.
The river flows with such élan,
The sun-filled azure skies.

A gentle wind flows through the trees.
Its leaves shift to and fro.
Swaying, silent melodies,
A breathless picture show.

The air is cool and clean and clear,
The hummingbird at feed.
The utter quiet draws me near.
I'm part of it, indeed.

As I view this peaceful play,
I'm filled with faith and calm.
This magic moment, dazzling day
Draws me to nature's arm.

Darwin termed it happenstance,
Science would agree.
Could it all be just by chance?
Not a chance for me.

Take the time if you've the nerve.
Stroll from sand to sea.
Seek your soul, unwind, observe
Your faith will set you free.

—Leonard Milgraum

ℭ℞

Deep within gardens of my mind
Are plantings filled with pleasure and elation,
So much living beauty can one find
In the soil and springs of one's imagination.

Varied hues appear at one's command,
Melding with their evergreen surround,
Fruitful arbors fill this wonderland,
Hummingbirds and squirrels do abound.

The air is filled with fragrances galore,
A subtle scent to sooth each stressful soul.
Each gentle hum of music can restore
A balance that can make our spirit whole.

Come cultivate a garden on your own,
Deep within the caverns of your mind,
Trees and flowers waiting to be grown
Created with your own unique design.

—Leonard Milgraum

❧ Nature

The buzzing bee,
The thrashing sea,
All so perfect, peaceful, calm.

The endless plains,
Refreshing rains,
All so lovely, quiet, serene.

The eagle's soar,
The lion's roar,
All such beauty, splendor, warmth.

The endless space,
Oh, nature's grace.
All so awesome, fascinating.

The first fall leaves,
Fall from the trees,
Ah, nature—utmost beauty.

—Rena Milgraum

CR

I sense an early winter in the chill of autumn's air.
The sun is shining brightly, but cannot dispel despair.
Spring and summer seemed so brief each swift but
    precious hour,
The birds, the bees, the stalwart trees, the beauty of each
    flower,
The strolls along the silent sand, along the pristine seas,
Each day a priceless gift from God to fill our memories.
I'm thankful for this treasured time, I pray and say
Amen.
I'm lifted by the thought that soon the spring will come
    again.

—Leonard Milgraum

❧ Snow

An endless blanket of wintery white,
A sinless world, an empty one
Nothing more within my sight,
But mountains of nature, hills of beauty.

Like a new leaf turned over,
A blank world, a new one,
New beginnings, new promises,
A new universe, just begun.

—Rena Milgraum

❧ *Snow 2*

Sparkling, glittering, crystals of white,
Glinting, glistening, crystals of light,
Blowing, snowing, through the sky,
Falling, falling, through the night.

Running, rolling through the snow,
Snowballs, snowflakes, here they go,
Bringing white, to light the world,
Spreading light from head to toe.

—Rena Milgraum

❧

I find you in the springtime,
As the buds begin to rise,
As the trees begin to waken,
Rub the slumber from their eyes.

I find you in the summer,
In the scent of flowers' bloom,
In the majesty of nature,
In fresh-cut hay's perfume.

I find you in the autumn,
In the burst of colored hues,
In the gentle zephyred breezes,
In the multicolored views.

I find you in the winter,
With the snow upon the earth,
With the trees in hibernation,
Waiting for the spring's rebirth.

Your handiwork is everywhere,
Creations of the Lord.
I open up my heart to you
And faith is my reward.

—Leonard Milgraum

C3 A Tree

Branches reaching up to the sky,
Gnarled roots clutching moist earth,
Bumpy, scratchy bark as skin,
An ancient friend, a tree.

With eyes that witnessed hundreds of years,
And leaves that soak up golden rays,
With roots that grasp towards earth's hot core,
An ancient friend, a tree.

Starting as a tiny seed,
Into a giant cork or oak,
A piece of nature, a piece of history
An ancient friend, a tree.

—Rena Milgraum

ℭ *Nature 3*

It takes a while to appreciate nature,
It takes a while to appreciate wildlife,
It takes a while to appreciate your surroundings,
It takes a while to appreciate life.

Learn to live with your surroundings,
Learn to live with nature itself,
Learn to live with wildlife,
Learn to live with life itself.

—Rena Milgraum

○ꝛ *Nature 4*

Waters crashing on the shore,
Birds chirping to the Lord,
Eagles fly way overhead,
All of this is nature.

Tiny plants begin to grow,
In colors one would never know,
Spreading glee to all who see,
Learn to know all nature.

The deer that run across the hill,
The cat curled on the windowsill,
The rocky mounts and grass and trees,
Learn to love all nature.

—Rena Milgraum

❧ *Summer Cottage—Gaspereaux*

This place remains, unchanged, now thirty years
Since first I set my eyes upon its shore.
Its constant gentle waves, lick on the sands,
Whispering of peace and stillness,
Inviting the soul.

I first came here a lad of sixteen,
Hungry, lonely, agitated, yearning for love.
At that time, I believed a blessed mate
Could soothe my yearning, quiet my discontent.

It was a teenage ballad of love.
But love, like the constantly shifting ocean
That now I sit beside
Holds many secrets
And unfolds,
In its own unhurried pace,
To the soul that is ready.

Now, thirty years along the road,
I've seen much of love,
In different shades and different moods,
A wife, of eighteen years,
Our longing for and fear to trust,
Arguments, talking it through,
A work in progress,
Step by painful step, we grow.
Four children,
Each a wonder and a riddle,
Reaching to the depth of my soul,
Each a story to unfold.

As for my restless longing—
Changed, to some extent.
The meaning in my role
Gives some satisfaction,
Motivates and draws me back from despair,
Though some days it's hard...
So very hard.

I stand upon the bluff,
Absorbing the medicine of this place,
Surveying its red clay cliffs
Made redder by the setting sun.

The sun lying gently, to repose,
Behind a bank of dark clouds,
But in the sun's muted lights
Arises the greatest glory of the day.

Wisps of clouds, far above,
Casually strewn about,
Capture the embers of that gently setting sun,
Giving each cloud an orange glow from within,
More delicate than any painter's palette.
A scene, uncapturable by words or even pictures.

Perhaps the glory lies
In the vastness of the view
And in its wholeness—a world connected, united.
I turn, slowly, slowly revolving
And witnessing—
Lush grass, swaying slightly in the breeze,
Tops rocky cliffs.
Darkening blue of the sea,

Rippling with waves upon waves,
Back to the horizon.
My eye scans across the bay—
The curve of the beach,
Constantly sculpted by the waves,
In the distance, a finger of land reaches out,
With a white lighthouse perched on its tip,
Flashing, beginning its evening sentinel...
Continuing to turn,
I see clusters of pine trees, far and near...
Turning, turning, my eyes caressing the scene,
My gaze returns to the red cottage,
Housing my family.
I hear laughter,
Then someone crying
And someone is being scolded.
Up close, these sounds can be stressful, annoying,
But from here—
It is all a part of the wonder and wisdom of the world.
Turning, turning, unchanged and always changing,
Held in His hands,
As we grow
And seek for Him.

I look up, hoping to see more.
I stare at the clouds
I stare within the clouds—
Their delicate, luminous orange.
I see what I sensed, but did not see before,
The clouds are not the same,
Even from one moment to another.
The light within them shifts and flows,
A scene that is always new,
A delightful dance of light,

Kissed by the sun,
Grey and white, orange and yellow
Combine and wash over each other—
A flow of light,
A flow of life
For those with the patience to look.

Soon the stars will appear,
Spreading new lacey patterns through the sky.
Then the moon will rise over the ocean,
Casting a trail of shimmering orange light
Upon the waves,
Dancing a new dance.

Here, here is my home.
Not a here of place,
But a here of spirit—
A spirit I have always sought.
It is a home that can travel with me
It is a home that sets me free to love,
And to dance with the wonder
Within that red cottage.

—Michael Milgraum

❧ *Spring Night*

Cool spring night,
Soft streetlights,
Moonlit, starry skies.
All is far,
Distant cars
Whisper in disguise.

Eerie, still,
Siren shrill
Hovers by the ear.
Muffled mind
Leaves behind
Worries, wishes, fears.

Spring night peace
Brings release.
Tension drifts away.
Resting mind
Helps us find
Strength to fight next day.

—Michael Milgraum

∝ *Spring Morn*

Chirping morn,
As the dawn
Brings the sweet spring day.
Feeling light,
Sunrise bright,
Gold and orange play.

Something clear
Fills the air,
Energy alive.
Robins run
In the sun,
Busy, buzzing hive.

Children's play
Is the day,
Happy just to be.
Chirping song
Fills the dawn,
Frolicking and free.

—Michael Milgraum

❧ A Summer's Eve

The crickets are chirping, in melodious harmony,
Wishing the world a daily farewell.
The squirrels cease their running, their leaping, their
    bounding,
Whispering to all that night's coming near.

A full moon is showing, as the blue sky turns pink,
Watching the sunset, framed by tall trees,
A few birds are chirping their lullabies to the chicks,
The last bees are buzzing around radiant flowers.

A perfect time to reflect on the happenings of the day,
As every living thing settles down for the night.
The scene fills me with wonder and indescribable awe,
I am part of this world, this world is part of me.

—Rena Milgraum

CR

I have no canvas, I cannot paint,
So I use words and phrases,
So kindly silence your complaint—
The scene I see amazes.

The sun brings warmth and light and more.
It radiates a glow.
It sends out energy galore
In God's great picture show.

The sky alive from cloud to cloud,
The mystery that lies beyond,
The breezes hum their song out loud,
There's music in the river, bay and pond.

The growing trees—each breath to clean the air,
The flowers bloom—gifting us their scent,
The grasses gleam, the birds are everywhere,
The chipmunks add their chirp to this event.

I quietly imbibe the priceless drink,
Surrounded by this wonderland of bliss,
Lauding this great landscape, as I think
That somehow I am part of all of this.

—Leonard Milgraum

CONNECTION AND DISCONNECTION

"It is not good for man to be alone." —Genesis 2:18

☘

What is a woman? What is a man?
What is a baby? A child?
What is our yesterday? What is today?
What is a groom or a bride?

What is tomorrow or tomorrow's tomorrow?
What's a lifetime in His eyes?
What can we give that He does not yet have?
How can we fill up the skies?

The thing we can give is to *be* in His world
And gratefully receive what He gives.
To savor the seconds, to open our hearts
To feel and to trust and to live.

Yet how can I feel when there's been so much pain?
But why should we hide it away?
To look at the sunshine, while trapped in past rain
Is to lose all the warmth of today.

The truth is so simple—
A baby, a child, a man both when young and when old
Wants someone to hold him and someone to hold,
To warm him when he's feeling cold,
Wants someone to know him, to hear him, to care
For the joy or the pain that's inside,
Wants someone to listen or watch as he grows—
A mother, a father, a friend or a bride.

But we live without questions
And run towards a time
That we dream of, but never arrive.

We lock up the feelings
And squander the gift...the seconds of our precious lives.

And the questions, the questions, the questions get lost,
The questions He put in our souls.
Who are you, my husband? Who are you, my wife?
What can I do to help you be whole?

So who is this woman? Who is this man?
Who is this baby, our child?
Can we learn from our yesterday? Live in today?
Renew joy with you by my side.

—Michael Milgraum

❧

Every person on this planet earth
Is unique and yearning to succeed.
Patterned, programmed from our very birth
With a soul implanted as a seed,

Exhibiting so many timeless traits,
A mixture of all giving and of taking,
Amalgam of confusion, loves and hates,
An unfinished pastry half through its baking,

Each of us a single grain of sand,
A separate, spinning universe, as well,
Inhabitants upon a fruitful land,
Wasting precious time on show and tell.

A great potential limping through the dance,
A symphony unfinished, fearful, flawed.
How to succeed, awaken from our trance?
Open yourself to the sibilant song of the Lord.

—Leonard Milgraum

❧ *Family*

Family means time spent together, and fun,
Peaceful and happy, time for everyone,
Family means love, so deep and so true,
Family means something between me and you.

So nice and so happy, so true and so real,
Family means something you cannot reveal,
So good and so fine, so right and so strong,
Family means something you've known all along.

It's not something you see; it's something you feel,
It's something that's warm; it's something that's real.
It's not something you smell; it's something you know,
It's something that will always live and will always grow.

—Rena Milgraum

Ↄↄ

Worries come and worries go,
Like the wind, the rain, the snow,
But one thing you should always know—
True love remains.

Flowers bud and bloom and fade,
A start and end to each parade,
Still never ever be afraid,
True love remains.

A single spark, as souls combine,
A wondrous "we" from thine and mine,
An everlasting shining sun,
As twin souls meld into one.

Clouds will float while rivers flow,
Constant change in life's great show,
One thing shines eternal glow—
True love remains.

The sun will rise, the stars will shine.
The seas and sands embrace, combine.
It's all a part of God's design,
From mountain peak to distant plains,
Flesh doth perish, but true love remains.

—Leonard Milgraum

CR

Seasons come and seasons go,
Sometimes flowers, sometimes snow,
In an endless panoply,
Day to night and night to day.

On and on from eons past,
From great feasts to famine's fast,
Endless rain then heartless drought.
Do you even wonder what it's all about?

Every person strives and just proceeds,
Battles for their bread, their daily needs.
Few are happy, most resigned
Few can sense Him, most are blind.

Open up the window to your soul.
Start by learning we're not in control.
Scrape the misconceptions from your core.
Open to His majesty with awe.

Use your intuition to locate
The meaning that will lead you to that gate.
Sense His vibrant presence everywhere
Through holiness and reverence in prayer.

You can find Him in the mountains, the forests or the sea
Or a special golden moment as we love our families.
His glory lies beyond the finite mind
In seeking Him, it's you that He will find.

—Leonard Milgraum

॰୬

We had this family dinner,
Each exotic dish,
Beef and lamb and chicken,
Caviar and fish.

Everyone dressed formal,
Conversation blah,
Different gems of value,
Coffee and cigar.

An ostentatious repast,
Which left me with a chill.
My stomach fully loaded,
My soul felt hungry still.

—Leonard Milgraum

ର

I know your weariness, my friend
For I have been there too.
I've felt the darkness, senseless sighs,
The longing to renew.

I've known the desperate despair,
When all the wells ran dry,
When dreams ring empty, hope is thin,
My life, a bitter lie.

I grew up in the sunshine.
We'd celebrate in song.
We gave ourselves to laughter.
Our unity made us strong.

I like the lessons that I learned
Within that magic space.
It taught the purity of the soul—
Eternal, sacred place.

But then the walls came crashing down,
As in growing up they must.
And I faced my first real challenge—
Who *outside* do I dare trust?

I could not trust the lot of them.
It was too much to bear.
They challenged me and all I knew.
They brought a dreadful fear.

And so I built the walls again,
And soon the walls built me.

They made me used to dull restraint
And choosing not to see.

The walls created two of me—
An inside and an out;
One confident enough to move,
One frozen, lost in doubt.

One talking with a steady voice,
One screaming from the pain,
One smiling, mouthing pleasantries,
One panicking, insane.

But, no! That was my worst mistake—
To call one part insane
And then protect the other part—
I built the wall again.

And so I built up many walls,
And with each wall, a voice
Grew up in strident chattering—
Cacophony of noise.

It was in this deep darkness,
Confused and lost I crawled,
Until I came upon the truth—
THE INSANITY WAS THE WALL.

Now, walls of mind grow over time,
They are not wished away,
And hitting them with angry fists,
Makes them more apt to stay.

So do not hate your walls, my friend,
If you wish to explore.
Just grab your tools and start to build
A window and a door.

The window lets the light come in
And helps you hear the song,
To see the friends, to smell the hope.
It helps to make you strong

To venture out beyond the door,
Though tentative you go,
You see firsthand what you have missed.
You see the sunrise glow.

I pray to find you there, my friend,
To hold your hand in mine,
To walk with you in whispered tones,
Our hearts and souls to find.

Don't be afraid, for growth takes time.
At times we'll want to hide.
At times we'll want to run away,
Or hold it all inside.

But I have found that wisdom beats
Within a living heart,
And with a will, there is a way
And with a dream, a start.

—Michael Milgraum

ℛ

Let's sing a song, a new song to the Lord,
To prize, to praise His truly great reward,
Alive with joy and gratitude,
An optimistic attitude.

Let's sing a song, a new song to the One
Who kindled first the flame within the sun,
Who makes the spring, the flowers bloom, the rivers
flow,
In time renews our water and our snow.

Let's mentally reenter Eden's gate,
Singing how we all appreciate,
The power of His presence, His holy majesty
His greatest gift—our very precious family.

Come sing a song, a new song to His name
To fill our hearts with happiness, free from fear and
    shame,
Free from stress and worries, following His way
Sing to praise each moment, each hour, every day.

—Leonard Milgraum

∝ Friends

Always there,
A perfect pair,
To reach out, and to guide you.

Never apart,
To touch your heart,
Smile, laugh and cry beside you.

Till the end,
A perfect friend,
To stumble, fall and climb with you.

Knowing you.
And what to do,
To love and live your life with you.

—Rena Milgraum

ॐ

It barely takes a moment
To make someone a friend—
A gentle smile, or soothing word,
A helping hand extend.

Or merely just to listen,
Absorb another's pain,
To care to make the effort,
To get one through the rain.

Remember someone's kindness
That helped you through a blight.
When someone's in the darkness
Your smile can bring the light.

Sometimes a simple gesture
May linger without end.
For it only takes a moment
To make someone a friend.

—Leonard Milgraum

☙ *Where Questions End*

The number one priority
Is that I know what I must be,
And so I spend confusing days
In analyzing all the ways
That I must act, if I be me,
Till all is one complexity.

But I'm a fool, for I know not
Of all the knowledge I have got,
And searching self, I've finally found
That in my searching I could drown.
The introspection's time is past.
It clutters more, the more it lasts.

There's so much more for me to see
In that great world outside of me,
And in the worlds inside of those
Who I've neglected, I suppose
I simply have not known, was blind,
To answers that were there to find.

But now I know the answers are
Not way beyond that distant star
Not pondering forevermore
Of what I have been put here for.
The answers lie within my reach
In all that I can learn and teach
With kindred souls outside my door.
That's what we both were put here for.

—Michael Milgraum

ॐ

Did you ever yearn to see
A preview of eternity,
A momentary glance or two
Of what may be in store for you?
There is a way to get you there—
Through reverence in prayer.

Your mind turns blank to all your woes,
And soon this feeling grows and grows.
You're filled with essence unrefined,
A harmony the Lord designed.
You float upon a magic stair—
Through reverence in prayer.

Just let the mundane muddle cease.
Open to your inner peace,
Employ a holy attitude,
And fill your heart with gratitude,
Banish guilt, disdain, despair—
Through reverence in prayer.

Make the words sincerely said.
Raise your soul and bow your head.
Chanting, humble in review,
Faith and love will see you through.
You can do it if you care—
Through reverence in prayer.

Disregard the pride parade.
Each of us can be remade.
Bring the noblest intent,
Every breath complete, content,

An elixir rich and rare—
Through reverence in prayer.

—Leonard Milgraum

ॐ

The silence still eludes me,
After searching all these years—
That simple, sweet serenity,
To get beyond the tears,
To get beyond the holding back,
The closing of the doors,
To leave behind the worry,
The anger and the wars.

And I know that I've been doing it;
The prison guard is me,
And yet the guard is ordered by
Someone I cannot see.
I do not know his nature,
But I sense that he is old,
Has served his job for eons now
By making warm things cold.

It is a tale of yin and yang,
Of dark revealing light,
Of limitation setting free,
And blindness brings in sight.
To find my home I left it,
To find the truth I lied.
I searched the world to find the place
That always was inside.

These things my teachers taught me,
And I believe they're true,
But now on cold, dark winter nights,
My heart yearns so for you.
And here's at last the pain of it—

I don't know who you are.
I only know the emptiness,
And that part of me is far.

Are you God, my spouse, a friend,
An innocent, childhood past,
A future where all things work out,
Where I'll find peace at last?
I really don't know who you are,
But I know you'd understand
My memories, my reveries,
My wandering, my plans.

I know that you would love me,
Would hold me till I sleep,
As mother comes to soothe the child,
When it begins to weep.
I know that you'd accept me,
Encourage me to thrive,
Would help me laugh a free, strong laugh,
Would make me feel alive.

I'm tired of the struggle,
So weary of the pain.
I want to find the you in me,
So I can live again.
I want to touch the world again,
To hear, to breathe, to see.
The demons—only love denied,
The jail, the key in me.

—Michael Milgraum

This poem is a reflection on the Amidah, a traditional Jewish prayer that is said in a whisper, while standing with the feet together. The sages say that one should stand this way during the prayer because we are imitating angels, who only have one leg.

℘ Amidah (As Angels Stand—In Stillness)

Our sages teach us how to stand and say,
Our whispered prayer before the holy One
That we should stand with both legs joined as one
To imitate the angels' single leg.
What does it mean that angels have one leg?
These beings of spirit without bodily form.
I think it means they know not human strife
Where heart fights mind, fights body, fights the soul.

The angels see the essence and the truth.
His will is never hidden from their sight,
While we must struggle, placed here in the world,
Where physicality can hide the One.
We human beings are by our nature split
And separated, seek to find the truth
And for the journey, God gives us two legs,
So we can move, and change and freely roam.

Our minds have legs and restlessly they run
To chart our course or find a better plan,
To find the answer, finish up the job,
So many jobs, we dizzy in the chase,
And so our sages have reminded us
To stop a moment our tormented minds,
To seek the soul of souls which surely knows
How angels stand, in stillness and in awe.

We seek not for escape but to recall,
The simple peace which helps us on our way,
To find the glory hidden in the world,
To find the courage to maintain our faith.
Each angel has one task, our sages say.
Uncomplicated beings the angels are.
So we should strive to find our special task
And do that task with a united heart.

Forgetting future fears and troubled past,
We find the present and find Him last.

—Michael Milgraum

ℭ

Listen to the music of the universe,
Learn to love its vibrancy and verve,
Sidestep pomp and preening,
Heed its special meaning,
Dare to dance the drama you deserve.

Listen to the music of the universe,
Cast aside depression and despair,
Hear its priceless words,
Soar beyond the birds,
Sing its precious message everywhere.

Listen to the music of the universe,
Each of us was chosen for our role,
Not to slump and brood,
Revise your attitude,
Reignite the rhythm in your soul.

Listen to the music of the universe,
Each of us is more than we conceive,
Don't let life's noise confuse us,
Let the Master's tunes infuse us,
Open to His wonders and achieve.

—Leonard Milgraum

CR

I lost my way one winter day.
I simply realized
That I'd been walking the wrong way,
Had lived too many lies.

I lived my days through arguments,
Debates inside my head.
I tried to be too good, too right,
And part of me felt dead.

My journey toward the truth,
I cannot say when it began,
But I have traveled many years
To strange, exotic lands.

You were also on a journey
On the day we met.
You sought for freedom, life and peace,
Beyond anger and regret.

Some live their lives in blindness
Some see, but do not care.
Some focus on externals
While running from despair.

Some others have the courage
To face their inner wars,
To see a truth to cleanse them,
Some have a soul like yours.

The challenge clear, I see, my dear,
To open up to you,

To share my pain, to find my joy,
To learn to love anew.

Sometimes I hide in fear and shame,
Afraid that you will see
The suffering and arguments,
Confusion, still in me.

I fear the contact just like you,
Yet know that when I see
A momentary glimpse of it,
Then for that moment, I am free.

Have patience, dear, and pray for me,
And I will pray for you.
You are my friend by now,
And more, you are my mirror too.

—Michael Milgraum

CR

Grant me endless clarity, oh Lord,
Righteousness of purpose and aim,
A giving self that will not hide or hoard,
The will to forage, feed and fan your flame.

I'll count my blessings each and every hour,
Then humbly stand and count them all once more,
Unfazed by petty pride or pompous power,
Do all I can to aid the frail and poor.

Sensing life's a testing interlude,
A stanza in a poem that never ends,
Feeding on our sacred texts like food,
Nourishing the soul as it ascends.

—Leonard Milgraum

◌ℛ *I'm Yearning to Live*

I want to climb the highest mountain,
I want to taste adventure,
I want to hear the cry of nature,
I want to be free, I want to live.

I want to explore the world's deepest secrets,
I want to be free to reach for the stars,
I want to smell the smell of calm,
Just let me be free, just let me live.

I want to understand life and its meaning,
I want to hold on to the memories of old,
I want to roar with the lion and soar with the eagle,
I'm yearning for freedom, I'm yearning to live.

—Rena Milgraum

CR

In the darkest of night,
You can still find a light,
A glow beyond sunrise of dawn.

In the depth of despair,
In your own soulful lair,
Lie the seeds to be smoothly reborn.

When it all falls apart,
If there's faith in your heart,
You'll discover your hidden abode.

With true love by your side,
There is no need to hide.
With courage to travel your road.

Simply straighten your spine,
Know your soul is divine.
You are more than the gold in your purse.

You are better by far
Than the world's brightest star.
You're a portion of God's universe.

—Leonard Milgraum

❧ Building onto God's Wonderful World

The laughter of children,
The rise and fall of ocean waves,
All beautifully intertwined,
All part of God's wonderful world.

The grace of nature,
How tranquil, how serene,
All perfectly set in its place,
All part of the canvas of God's flawless world.

The birth of a child,
Helpless, tiny and innocent,
As it journeys through life,
Building onto God's wonderful world.

—Rena Milgraum

Jewish tradition teaches that every man or woman has two forces that battle within them—a Yetzer Hatov (good inclination) and a Yetzer Hara (evil inclination). The sages warn that a person must be vigilant to the trickery of the Yetzer Hara and must hold fast to the straight and narrow path of discipline and goodness. However, the sages also teach that there is nothing *in this world that does not have a Godly-ordained purpose, even the Yetzer Hara. Without the temptation of the Yetzer Hara, man would be no more than a robot, programmed to follow the will of God. It is the temptation supplied by the Yetzer Hara that allows us to exercise free will and turn towards the good. By making this free-willed choice towards good, we earn eternal merit from God.*

◌ Yetzer Hara

He comes with silent creeping,
A sly and cunning hand.
In darkness he stays crouching,
He watches, waits and plans.

He'll trick you, trip you, trap you.
He'll whisper in your ear,
Your very best intentions.
Your reasoning sound and clear.

He dresses up our hatred,
Our selfishness, rage and greed,
In webs of rationalizations
And calls them righteous deeds.

He takes our normal hunger
For food, strength, loving trust,
Contorting them into gluttony.
And bullying and lust.

To the fearful he shows images
Of danger, suffering, death.
While the rageful hear derision,
Which fuels their angry breath.

To those who are addicted
He says, "One more drink, that's all."
To those who play the victim
He says, "The other made you fall."

To each of us our weakness,
In each of us a crack,
When we try to escape him,
He grabs us, pulls us back.

He thrives within the darkness.
He feeds upon our lies.
He lives upon our deadening.
His conquers through disguise.

And yet he's just a servant
To Someone good and grand—
A loving living Presence
Who holds us in His hands.

The grand One tries and tests us,
He hides that we may seek,
Deprives us, so we yearn for more,
Goes far, that we may reach.

A reach beyond the darkness,
Above this endless fight,
Where demons can't torment us

And with new eyes we see the truth—
A world that's bathed in light.

—Michael Milgraum

CR

On starry night I gaze above,
And look forever in the eye—
A universe of empty space
I give a deep, soul-searching sigh.

Eternal width, eternal length,
A distance I can't comprehend.
I'm face to face with infinite
A journey that could never end.

The stars defy a limit too.
Their faces light the evening sky
With trillions looking down on me,
They sparkle sweetly from on high.

Yet "sweetly" isn't quite the word;
Sometimes they seem remote to me—
A stern reminder by my Lord
Of how our world was meant to be.

He wants for me to understand,
He gives to me the clearest sign
That though our earth might seem unique,
I have no right to call it mine.

'Tis part of all that I survey,
Which does not make it seem more small.
No, it becomes a crucial brick
In a majestic shining wall.

And so the same is true for me,
For though I'll always be one man,

I'll also be a vital tool
To carry out God's sacred plan.

—Michael Milgraum

છ

I seek a magic carpet
To fly me to the sun.
I miss a long-lost childhood
When all was fresh and young.

A slow and plodding vessel
Is body for the soul.
The soul has dreams and visions
Untiring in its goal.

The body goes more slowly,
Adjusting so to grow,
Digesting, ruminating
With lumbering steps we go.

I see the bright young toddler
With spirit swift as wind,
But all the same, to rise, to walk
He tries, fails, tries again.

There is a difference 'tween he and me—
Despondent I stumble along,
But "failure" does not daunt his will,
He laughs, he smiles, so strong.

I must embrace this plodding child
Or I'll despair each day,
For though the soul can soar, can fly,
The body builds runways.

And more than that, the body gives me
Wings to soar toward the sun.

'Tis in the dance of body-soul
That we find all is one.

We're all a part of one big soul.
Each flying toward the light.
Some go too fast, get burnt in flames
While others hide in fright.

But if we'd have the courage,
Like that child, to rise again,
We'd find the secrets that he knows—
The universe his friend.

—Michael Milgraum

❧ Dusk of Childhood—Dawn of Man

I stand alone in a darkening field,
Listening to the sounds of approaching night,
Feeling the damp, cool, air,
Shivering a little—from the air,
Or perhaps from the thoughts that seem
To float in the air.
A world is fading fast;
I am alone,
Staring at a star,
Just as a being that was not quite a man
Must have stood here eons ago
Staring upwards—over glistening swampland and trees,
Over the horizon of fading gold,
Towards one solitary star.
I can see him so clearly—
Furrowed brow, sloping forehead, curved posture,
Heavy, dull face,
But questioning eyes,
Wondering what is born in the golden sunset,
Watching his star,
Our star...for he is me.
I shiver, shake my head,
But the picture does not go away.
We wrinkle our foreheads.
Gaze more intently,
Begin to wonder
About things to which we can give no name,
Things that seem to be beyond that star.
Yes, we stand—
My prehistoric friend
And a million other spirits within me.
I carry them past the star

Through the golden horizon
That shines through the sea of trees
Above the darkened field,
Bidding farewell to this day,
Wondering at the promise of tomorrow.

—Michael Milgraum

ॐ

So many people make themselves ill,
Then seek a solution with powder or pill.
They continue to languish in deep yesteryear,
Cornered and captured by fanciful fear.
Created we were to be good and be grand.
Resolution resides in your very own hand...

Open yourself to a soft scented breeze,
Simply release all the dank memories,
Quietly search for the message inside,
Bypass the ego, the anguish and pride.

Sort through your baggage, the pain in the past.
Write a new drama—choose your own cast.
Discard the detritus, compose a new show.
Solve all your problems, by just letting go.

—Leonard Milgraum

www.ingramcontent.com/pod-product-compliance
Lightning Source LLC
Chambersburg PA
CBHW060746100426
42813CB00032B/3420/J